Worldly Difficulties

Reality | Consolation
Causes | for the
Benefits | Grieving Heart

Compiled by Shawana A.Aziz

D1620476

Contents

بِسْمِ اللَّهِ الرَّحْمَنِ الرَّحِيمِ

About the
Book

Worldly difficulties are an inevitable part of life; they range from simple problems to fatal diseases and loss of loved ones. This booklet helps the reader see his arduous affairs in their appropriate perspectives by encouraging complete trust in Allah's Decisions, and by defining the great principle of *al-Qadha wal-Qadar* (Predestination) that, 'Whatever happened to you, could not have missed you.'

This booklet reminds the reader that worldly difficulties are a trial for the believers, while not disregarding the fact that more often afflictions result from one's sins and disobedience to Allah.

This booklet also teaches how appropriate behavior and correct attitude can change an adversity into a worthwhile opportunity to achieve Allah's Pleasure through *Sabr, Shukr, Ihtisaab* and *Istirja*, whereas impatience, panic and complaining can worsen one's state of affairs.

Finally, this booklet explains the futility of invoking the Prophets and the dead to remove hardships, and encourages calling upon Allah Alone to ease one's affairs.

I hope that this booklet will bring solace and comfort to people as they struggle to manage the difficulties of life. I ask Allah to accept this humble effort and all success is from Allah.

Shawana A. Aziz

Life of the world is a trial

Disbelievers see afflictions as mere inconvenience; but for the believers, hardships are a trial and an opportunity to strengthen one's bond with the Lord. Allah, the Exalted, tests His slaves with calamities and blessings. If the believer endures the calamity with patience, Allah, the All Merciful, rewards him abundantly, expiates his sins and elevates his ranks in Jannah. "Surely We will test you with fear, hunger, loss of wealth and life and the fruits of your work, but give glad tidings to the patient - those who, when afflicted with a calamity say, 'to Allah we belong and to Him we shall return.' Those are the ones upon whom are bestowed blessings and mercy from their Lord, and those are the ones who are (truly) guided." [Soorah al-Baqarah (2): 155]

On the other hand, disbelievers are truly at a loss because they have no hope of being rewarded for their perseverance or patience. Allah says, "...if you are suffering (hardships) then surely, they (too) are suffering (hardships) as you are suffering, but you have a hope from Allah (for the reward, i.e. Paradise) that for which they hope not..." [Soorah an-Nisa (4): 104]

The following pages define in light of the Qur'aan and the guidance of Allah's Messenger ﷺ how a believer can reap the most benefit from his hardships through appropriate behavior and attitude.

Complete trust in Allah's decision

It is an integral part of a Muslim's Faith (Eemaan) to believe that everything Allah chooses for him; good or evil, pleasure or affliction, is for the slave's benefit. The Messenger of Allah ﷺ said, "By Him, in Whose Hand is my soul, Allah does not ordain a Decree for a believer but for his good; and this merit is for no one except a believer..." [Saheeh Muslim]

It is beyond human understanding to completely comprehend the Divine Wisdom behind every affliction because our knowledge is limited only to the apparent event. Allah Alone knows how things will turn out in the end, and how it will benefit the slave. So, the calamity that appears to be evil may lead to many favorable benefits. Allah says in the Qur'aan, "...it may be that you dislike a thing which is good for you and that you like a thing which is bad for you. Allah knows (what is best for you) and you do not." [Soorah al-Baqarah (2): 216]

One must therefore, always expect good from Allah and trust His Decision and Judgment with regard to every aspect of his life. Allah has promised that if the believers show reliance in their Lord, then Allah will suffice them, "Whoever trusts in Allah, will find

Him sufficient. Verily, Allah will accomplish His purpose." [Soorah at-Talaq (65): 3]

The Qur'aan gives us the example of Prophet Yaqub's ﷺ strong trust in Allah. He ﷺ had very handsome children. When he sent his children to Egypt; he instructed them to enter Egypt through different gates because he feared evil eye for them. "And he said, 'O my son! Do not enter by one gate, but enter by different gates…" and then he ﷺ says, "…I cannot avail you against Allah. The decision rests only with Allah. I put my trust in Him alone, and all who trust should only trust Him." [Soorah Yusuf (12): 67] Meaning although my precaution cannot prevent Allah's Decision and appointed Decree; I trust in Allah that whatever He chooses will be the best.

The Messenger of Allah ﷺ explained that the believer should always be satisfied with the Decree of Allah. He should be pleased and thankful to Allah when he is granted ease and pleasure of life, and he should practice patient when calamities afflict him. He ﷺ said, "…If he (the believer) is granted ease of living, he is thankful; and this is best for him. And if he is afflicted with a hardship, he perseveres; and this is best for him." [Saheeh Muslim]

It is prohibited to show impatience, or extreme excitement, anger, or do actions or say words which might show dissatisfaction with Allah's Decree, like wailing, tearing clothes, slapping cheeks, etc. One will be held accountable on the Day of Judgment for all prohibited acts that he is capable of avoiding. Imam al-Bukharee (rahimahullah) has recorded in his Saheeh from Abu Musa al-Ansari that the Prophet ﷺ has declared himself free from him who wails at the time of affliction, one who shaves the head at the time of affliction (as an act of expressing grief), and the one who tears clothes at the time of affliction. All such acts are forbidden according to the consensus of the scholars.

Allah, however, does not punish His slaves for actions that are beyond his control. For example, one does not have much control over tears and emotions of the heart. One may experience sorrow and grief due to loss of something cherished or departure of one's beloved. Allah will not punish the slave for the tears and sorrow of the heart, but it is necessary for the slave to dislike every evil thought that crosses his mind and prevent the tongue from saying anything which may express displeasure with Allah's Decree. Allah's Messenger ﷺ visited his companion, Sa'd Ibn Ubadah, who was ill and along with him were some of his Companions. Allah's Messenger ﷺ wept on seeing Sa'd Ibn Ubadah and when the others saw him weep they also wept. The Prophet ﷺ then said, "Listen! Allah does not punish due to the tears of the eyes or the sorrow of the heart, but He punishes because of this (and he pointed to his tongue) or He shows mercy." [Saheeh al-Bukharee]

When Ibraheem, the son of Allah's Messenger ﷺ, was at his last breath, he ﷺ went to him and his eyes filled with tears. Abdur-Rahman Ibn Auf ؓ said to him, "Even you, O Messenger of Allah ﷺ (weep)!" The Prophet ﷺ replied, "O Ibn Auf, it is mercy." Then he wept some more, and said, "The eye weeps and the heart sorrows and we do not say anything except what is pleasing to our Lord. By your leaving, O Ibraheem, we are sorrowed." [Saheeh al-Bukharee]

whatever happened to you could not have missed you

Nothing takes place on earth, except that it is inscribed in al-Lawh al-Mahfoodh or 'the Preserved Tablet,' where Allah, the Exalted, has recorded everything about the creation; livelihood, provisions, ages, deeds, etc. The Messenger of Allah ﷺ said, "Allah had written the ordained measures (and due proportions) of the creation, fifty-thousand years before the creation of the Heavens and the Earth..." [Saheeh Muslim]

Similarly, every calamity that befalls the slave has been pre-ordained by Allah. "No disaster strikes upon the earth or within yourselves but was recorded in a Book (al-Lawh al-Mahfoodh) before We bring it into existence. Verily, this is easy for Allah..." [Soorah Hadid (57): 22-23]

Allah states the wisdom behind pre-ordainment (in the next verses of Soorah Hadid) that the slave should neither despair if calamity afflicts, nor become proud and haughty on achieving good; because every calamity that befalls him was previously designated for him and all blessings are due to Allah's Favor and Mercy. So, whatever reached him could not have missed him and whatever missed him could not have reached him. This belief is an essential part of Eemaan (faith), when Allah's Messenger ﷺ was asked: "What is Eemaan?" He ﷺ replied, "Eemaan is to believe in Allah, His Angels, His Books, His Messengers, the Last Day and to believe in Predestination; the good and the bad." [Agreed upon]

The slave should also refrain from over speculation and conjecture, like saying, 'If I had done such and such... the result would have been different...' or '...I would have been saved from this calamity...' etc. The Messenger of Allah ﷺ said, "...and if anything (in the form of trouble) comes to you, don't say, 'if I had not done that, it would not have happened so and so,' but say, Allah did what He had ordained and your 'if' opens the gate for Shaytan." [Saheeh Muslim (6441)]

Allah, the Exalted, has promised to grant tranquility and guide the hearts of the believers if they refrain from speculation. Allah says, "No disaster strikes except by Allah's Permission, and whoever believes in Allah, He guides his heart, Allah is the Knower of all things." [Sorah Taghabun (64):11] Ibn Abbas ؓ said Allah's guiding the heart of the slave means that Allah will guide his heart to certainty. Therefore, he will know that what reached him would not have missed him, and what has missed him would not have reached him. [Tabari 23:421]

Imam Ibn Katheer (rahimahullah) writes in his Tafseer, "...after suffering from an affliction, if the slave believes that it occurred by Allah's Judgment and Decree, and he patiently abides, awaiting Allah's reward, then Allah guides his heart and will compensate him for his loss in this life by granting guidance to his heart and certainty in faith. Allah will replace whatever he lost with the equal or what is better."

Afflictions
are a
form of
blessing

Apart from some hardships, afflictions also bring about various benefits for the believer. Recognizing them makes easy the path of patience and endurance for the believer;

● Hardships teach the believer to be patient and Allah abundantly rewards His patient slaves.

● Sufferings remind the sinful believer about the greatest affliction of life, i.e. death, which may afflict him at any moment. It reminds him of the severe punishments, which may follow next, as a result of his disobedience to Allah.

When one deviates, he seldom pays any heed to the advice of others; but when calamity strikes, he is reminded of Allah and His severe punishments. Allah says, "We will make them taste a lesser punishment before the greater punishment that perhaps they may return (to the right path)." [Soorah as-Sajdah (32): 2] So, calamities give one the time to reflect over one's sins and their awful outcome. As a result, one recognizes his errors and returns to Allah in repentance; worldly difficulties thus, serve as a blessing for the sinful.

● Hardships reduce the burden of sins from the believer freeing him from the severe and unbearable punishments of the Hereafter. The Messenger of Allah ﷺ said, "Afflictions continue to befall believing men and women in their body, family and property, until they meet Allah burdened with no sins." [as-Saheehah (2280)] and he ﷺ also said, "No stress or exhaustion befalls the Muslim, nor worry or distress, even a thorn which pricks him, but Allah will expiate his sins because of that." [Agreed upon]

Suffering in this world is insignificant in comparison to the harsh unbearable punishments of the Hereafter. Besides, death puts an end to a person's suffering in this world, whereas punishments of the Hereafter are eternal!

Moreover, Allah forgives most of our disobedience in the world, and what we suffer of the hardships is a retribution for only a fraction of our sins. Allah, the All-Merciful, informs us in the Qur'aan, "Whatever befalls you is a result of what your hands have earned. And He (Allah) pardons much." [Soorah ash-Shura (42): 30]

If we were to be punished for all of our evil deeds, everything on the Earth be destroyed. Allah says in Soorah Fatir, "if Allah were to punish men for that which they earned, He would not leave a moving (living) creature on the face of the Earth, but He gives respite for an appointed term..." [Soorah Faatir (35): 45]

So, it is from the immense Mercy of Allah that He pardons

much of our evil deeds and He has made the afflictions of this life an atonement for the harsh and severe punishments of the Hereafter. Allah's Messenger ﷺ said: "When Allah wills good for a servant of His, He expedites his punishments in this life, and when He wills retribution for a servant of His, He holds his sins for him to judge him by them on the Day of Judgment." [Saheeh al-Jamee (308)]

● Hardships establish submission and humbleness in the believer; for instance, when afflicted with sickness, the slave realizes his weakness and need for Allah; and he invokes His Lord for good health; and after having been granted fitness, he becomes thankful to His Lord for alleviating his hardships and strives harder in worshiping Him.

Had he always lived a healthy life without having experienced any difficulty or hardship, he would have grown arrogant and proud. Likewise, if he were to be ill all the time, he would not have had the opportunity to worship Allah and be grateful to Him.

These and many other benefits of worldly difficulties together bring about numerous blessings for the believer. Besides, worldly difficulties are necessary for the spiritual growth of the believer since they purify him from sins, help him worship Allah sincerely and establish his Deen (religion). It is for this reason that the Prophets ﷺ and their followers were pleased when afflicted with hardships. Allah's Messenger ﷺ said, "The Prophets are afflicted the most, then the righteous. Indeed, one of them would be tested with poverty, so that he would not be able to wear anything except a coarse cloak. And indeed, they used to be pleased with affliction as you are with comfort." [as-Saheehah (144)]

The believer
should NOT
wish for
calamites

It might seem appropriate to wish and endure worldly difficulties in return for the various benefits, rewards and freedom from the punishments of the Hereafter; but the believer is prohibited from wishing for calamities.

Firstly because one is likely to fall into ingratitude and disbelief at the time of difficulties. Moreover, it is not possible for anyone to endure the punishment of his sins in this life.

Secondly, wishing for calamities would conflict with the easy and forgiving nature of Islam. We are instructed to ask for our well being and forgiveness. Allah, the Exalted, has taught this prayer in the Qur'aan,

رَبَّنَا لَا تُؤَاخِذْنَا إِن نَّسِينَا أَوْ أَخْطَأْنَا رَبَّنَا وَلَا تَحْمِلْ عَلَيْنَا إِصْرًا كَمَا حَمَلْتَهُ عَلَى الَّذِينَ مِن قَبْلِنَا رَبَّنَا وَلَا تُحَمِّلْنَا مَا لَا طَاقَةَ لَنَا بِهِ وَاعْفُ عَنَّا وَاغْفِرْ لَنَا ارْحَمْنَا

"Our Lord! Punish us not if we forget or fall into error,
Our Lord! Lay not on us a burden like that which You did lay
on those before us (Jews and Christians);
Our Lord! Put not on us a burden greater
than we have strength to bear.
Pardon us and grant us Forgiveness. Have mercy on us."
[Soorah al-Baqarah (2): 286]

So, the believer should take advantage of Allah's Mercy and ask His forgiveness. Anas ♦ reported that Allah's Messenger ♦ once visited a Muslim man who was so weak that he was (thin) like a chicken, as described in the Hadeeth. Allah's Messenger ♦ asked him, "Did you make a specific supplication or ask Allah for something (because of which you became like this)?" He replied, "Yes, I used to say, 'O Allah! Whatever punishment you have for me in the Hereafter, expedite it for me in this life." Allah's Messenger ♦ said, "Exalted be Allah! You cannot withstand that. Instead, you should have said,

"Our Lord, grant us good in this life and in the next life,
and protect us from the punishment of the Fire."
[Soorah al-Baqarah (2): 201]

He ♦ then implored Allah to cure him, and Allah cured him."
[Saheeh Muslim]

If Allah grants ease...

The believer should be thankful to Allah if he is granted ease and comfort. However, one should not deem ease of life to be a result of one's piety and righteousness because worldly difficulties are not the only trials of the world. Rather, prosperity, wealth and well being are also part of the test. Allah says, "...And We shall make a trial of you with evil and with good..." [Soorah al-Ambiya (21): 35] meaning, We shall test you sometimes with difficulties and sometimes with ease, to see who will give thanks and who will be ungrateful, who will be patient and who will despair.

Ali Ibn Abi Talib ﷺ reported from Ibn Abbas ﷺ that Allah will test you with difficulties and with times of prosperity, with health and sickness, with richness and poverty, with lawful and unlawful, obedience and sin, with guidance and misguidance." [See Tafseer Ibn Katheer]

blessing or punishment

While patience and submission in times of difficulty can bring rewards and blessings for the believer; displeasure and impatience can incur Allah's Wrath and Punishment on the slave. Allah's Messenger ﷺ said, "The magnitude of the reward is in accordance with the magnitude of the affliction. When Allah loves some people, He afflicts them. He who is then content (with Allah's Decree) will achieve the acceptance (of Allah); and he who is dissatisfied (with Allah's Decree) will attain the anger (of Allah)." [Saheehah (146)] So, it rests upon the slave; either he seizes the opportunity of achieving Allah's Pleasure or faces misery.

Towards achieving Allah's **Pleasure** and **Blessing**

Sabr

'Sabr' is an Arabic word coming from a root that means, 'to detain, refrain and stop.' In the Islamic terminology, 'Sabr' means, 'to stop oneself from despairing and panicking; to stop the tongue from complaining, and to stop the hands from striking the face and tearing the clothes at a time of grief and distress.'

Those who possess the quality of 'Sabr' are indeed blessed, for Allah's Messenger ﷺ is reported to have said, "No one is given anything better and more encompassing than patience." [Saheeh al-Bukharee]

Allah, the Exalted, has promised for the Saabiroon (those who show Sabr) abundant reward that will not be weighed or measured! He said, "Only those who are patient shall receive their rewards in full, without reckoning." [Soorah az-Zumar (39): 10]

True Sabr that will bring about the promised reward has to be practiced at the beginning of the calamity, when one first hears the news of affliction. In spite of the heart's sorrows, the slave does not panic or despair. He exhibits patience and satisfaction with the Decree of Allah.

Patience after the initial shock when the grief has reduced is not true Sabr. The real test of patience is at the time when one is grieved by the calamity. The Prophet ﷺ said, "Verily patience is at the first hit (of news)." [Saheeh al-Bukharee]

Every person practices patience, willingly or unwillingly. The wise person is he who practices patience willingly and from the beginning because he understands the benefits of patience. He knows that he will be rewarded for his patience and will be criticized if he panics. He is aware that impatience and despair can neither bring back missed opportunities nor change the Decree of Allah.

Foolish is he who practices patience only after having complained and shown anguish and he cannot find any other choice. Sabr at this point does no good.

Towards achieving Allah's **Pleasure** and **Blessing**

Ihtisaab

'Looking forward to Allah's reward and forgiveness for every affliction, regardless of the pain and suffering' is called Ihtisab. Allah's Messenger ﷺ said, "When Allah takes away from His believing servant his beloved one of the people of the earth; if he displays patience and Ihtisab, Allah will then not accept any reward for him less than Jannah (Paradise)." [Saheeh al-Bukharee]

Let us take the example of Aasiyah, the wife of Firawn. Aasiyah was severely tortured by her husband, who was a king, because she had accepted the Oneness of Allah. In spite of the severe anguish and pain, Aasiyah persisted in her faith, displayed immense patience and practiced Ihtisab. She prayed to Allah and asked Him for a home in Paradise. Allah mentions her story in the Qur'aan, "And Allah has set forth an example for those who believe, the wife of Firawn, when she said, "My Lord! Build for me a home with You in Paradise and save me from Firawn and his work, and save me from the people who are wrongdoers." [Soorah at-Tahrim (66): 11]

When she invoked Allah with this du'a, the sky opened for her and she saw her home in Paradise. She smiled. Firawn commanded a big rock to be brought and dropped on Aasiyah in order to crush her to death. But Allah took her soul before the rock was dropped. So, Allah granted Aasiyah two blessings for her Ihtisab; a home in Paradise and protection from the cunning plans of Firawn. She is thus an example for all those who will come after her until the Day of Judgment. [See at-Tabari 23: 500]

Towards achieving Allah's **Pleasure** and **Blessing**

Istirja

Expressing Allah's Lordship and submission to His Decree by words, i.e. saying,

إِنَّا لِلَّهِ وَإِنَّا إِلَيْهِ رَاجِعُونَ

'Indeed, we belong to Allah,
and indeed to Him we shall return.'

Allah says, "Surely, We will test you with fear, hunger, loss of wealth and life and the fruits of your work but give glad tidings to the patient - those who, when afflicted with a calamity say, "Inna lillahi wa Inna Ilaihi Raji'un." Those are the ones upon whom are bestowed blessings and mercy from their Lord, and those are the ones who are (truly) guided." [Soorah al-Baqarah (2): 155-7]

Umm Salamah (radhi allahu anha) reported that she heard Allah's Messenger ﷺ say, "Whenever an affliction strikes a believer and he says,

إِنَّا لِلَّهِ وَإِنَّا إِلَيْهِ رَاجِعُونَ اللَّهُمَّ أُجُرْنِي
فِي مُصِيْبَتِي وَاخْلُفْ لِي خَيْراً مِنْهَا.

"Inna lillahi wa Inna Ilaihi Raji'un.
Allahum majurni fi musibati wakhluf li khayran minha."

"Indeed, we belong to Allah,
and indeed to Him we will return.
O Allah! Reward me for my calamity,
and replace it for me that which is better."

Allah will surely reward him for it and replace it for him with a better thing." Umm Salamah (radhi allahu anha) added, "So, when Abu Salamah (her husband) died, Allah enabled me to say this (du'a), and He replaced him for me with Allah's Messenger ﷺ." [Saheeh Muslim]

Shakwah

Shakwah (complaining) falls into two categories;

(a) The first type is to complain to Allah and this does not contradict patience. A number of examples of Shakwah to Allah can be found in the Qur'aan, one of which is the complaining of Yaqub عليه السلام, who said, "I complain of my distraction and anguish to Allah." [Soorah Yusuf (12): 86]

(b) The second type of Shakwah involves complaining to people, either directly through words or indirectly through the way we look and behave, like dressing shabbily, shaving the head, displaying distress, etc. all in order to show one's grief and pain. This type of Shakwah is contradictory to Sabr because it implies disagreeing with Allah's Decree and lack of trust in Him.

One may, however, mention his suffering to some people like close friends. Ibn Mas'oud رضي الله عنه reported that he visited the Prophet ﷺ when he was sick; he touched him with his hand, and felt the fever. He said, "You have a severe fever." He replied, "Yes, I suffer from fever as much as would two men among you!" [Agreed upon]

another aspect
of worldly difficulties!

We understand from the discussions on the previous pages that worldly difficulties are a trial, during which the believer is required to be patient and submit to Allah's Decree. But more often afflictions are also a result of the believer's sins and evil deeds. They are a punishment from Allah and a warning to shun evil deeds and return back to Allah in repentance. "Whatever of misfortune befalls you is a result of what your hands have earned." [Soorah ash-Shura (42): 30]

It is very important to clearly understand this aspect of worldly difficulties and give it due consideration. The Qur'aan is a witness that Allah severely punished and subsequently destroyed the past nations who did not pay heed to His admonitions and warnings. He punished the disbelievers at the time of Noah ﷺ with a terrible flood. He decided to send an awful wind storm upon the people of Hud ﷺ as a penalty. A disastrous earthquake destroyed the arrogant at the time of Salih ﷺ. The people of Lut were turned upside down and stones of baked clay rained on them ... These and other stories of the past nations warn us about the bad consequences of disobeying Allah and disregarding His admonitions, Allah says, "Let those who contradict his (the Messenger's

- 22 -

⛭) command beware of a trial or a severe punishment." [Soorah an-Nur (24): 63]

Punishments can be in various forms. Perhaps, today what seems the most obvious punishment afflicting mankind is AIDS, which appeared for the first time in the 80's. AIDS is a fatal disease that weakens the resistance of body and makes it defenseless against all kinds of infections. Anyone who develops AIDS dies within a few years. AIDS is spread mainly due to indiscriminate sexual activity, homosexuality and drug abuse, all of which are actions that transgress the limits of Allah.

Some may argue that AIDS is not limited to sinful people but has also spread among the chaste individuals. The Qur'aan gives the reply that when the punishment of Allah befalls, it does not only besiege the sinful, but afflicts the society as a whole. Allah says, "Beware of a trial which will not afflict only the sinful among you, and know that Allah is severe in punishment." [Soorah Anfal (8): 25]

AIDS is only one in the series of calamities and adversities afflicting mankind. Today, we hear of a number of diseases, unexpected storms, floods and earthquakes afflicting different parts of the world. Punishing reminders also come in the form of oppression from the enemy. This is a result of our disobedience to Allah that we are surrounded by hardships and adversities.

Allah is warning us. Know that the only solution is to refrain from violating the laws of Allah and restricting oneself within the bounds of Islam. The Qur'aan says, "Corruption has appeared on the land and in the sea because of what man's hands have earned in order that (Allah) may make them taste a part of what they have done, and in order that they may return (to the right path)." [Soorah ar-Rum (30):41]
We should greatly consider these warnings and hasten towards repentance, and depart from all such acts, which may become the cause of our destruction. We should work towards righteousness and please our Lord before it is too late - and before we get caught up in punishments that become difficult for us to escape.

Calling
upon Allah
alone

in times of afflictions

How unfortunate are those who, when afflicted with difficulty and hardship run towards tombs and graves in search of help and relief. They are found invoking the Prophets ﷺ and the dead to dispel hardships. Allah says about them, "And who is more astray than one who calls (invokes) besides Allah, such as will not answer him till the Day of Resurrection, and who are (even) unaware of their calls (invocations) to them?" [Soorah al-Ahqaf (46): 5]

It would be enough to mention only one Hadeeth of Allah's Messenger ﷺ to prove the futility of their action. Allah's Messenger ﷺ said, "Those who are most afflicted among the people are the Prophets, then the best, then the (next) best. One is afflicted in accordance with (the strength of) his Deen. If his Deen is firm, his affliction is hard, and if his Deen is weak, his affliction is light. Indeed, one would be so much subjected to adversity until he walks among the people without any sin." [Saheeh al-Jamee (993)]

Apart from explaining that Prophets are afflicted the most, then the best and then the best, this Hadeeth is a proof of Tawheed (Oneness of Allah). If one knows that the Prophets and the righteous people are also afflicted with calamities and they suffer more than the common believers and that none can remove these afflictions from them except Allah - Then he will completely understand that when they cannot bring benefit nor prevent harm from their ownselves - how could they ward off evil from others? Consequently, it is established that turning towards the Prophets and Awliya (righteous) to alleviate one's distress is futile and hopeless, rather one should turn towards Allah, who Alone dispels all harm.

Allah mentions the story of Prophet Ayub ﷺ, who was tested with regard to his wealth, children, and physical health. He had plenty of livestock, cattle and crops, many children and beautiful houses, and he was tested when he lost everything he possessed. Then he was tested with regard to his body, and he was left alone on the edge of the city, no one to treat him except his wife. But Prophet Ayub ﷺ had the utmost patience and trust in Allah; thus he invoked Allah alone for help, "And remember Ayub when he cried to his Lord, 'Verily, distress has seized me, and You are the Most Merciful of all those who show mercy." [Soorah al-Ambiya (21): 83] Allah says: "So, We answered his call, and we removed the distress that was on him, and We restored his family to him, and the like thereof with them as a mercy from ourselves and a reminder for all those who worship Us." [Soorah al-Ambiya (21): 84]

The Qur'aan clearly states that those who are dead cannot help the living. Therefore, anyone who calls upon the dead is surely a loser. Furthermore, invoking someone others besides Allah is committing Shirk (associating partners with Allah) the most evil crime because supplication is worship, and thus it is the Right of Allah Alone. Allah says, "Invoke Me and I will respond to your (invocation). Verily, those who scorn My worship, will enter Hell in humiliation." [(40): 60] While explaining this verse the Messenger of Allah ﷺ said, "Supplication is worship." [Sunan Abu-Dawood (1474)]

If the slaves secure the Right of Allah and worship Him Alone, then Allah has promised to save them from His punishments, and pardon their sins, as is known from the following Hadeeth. Narrated Muadh bin Jabal 🙲 that the Messenger of Allah 🙵 asked, "O Muadh! Do you know what is the Right of Allah on His slaves?" I (Muadh bin Jabal) said, "Allah and His Messenger 🙵 knows best." The Prophet 🙵 said, "(the Right of Allah on His slaves is) to worship Him (Allah) Alone and join none (as partners) in worship with Him." Then he 🙵 asked, "Do you know what is their (slaves) right upon Him?" I replied, "Allah and His Messenger 🙵 knows best." The Prophet 🙵 said, "Not to punish them (if they worship Him alone)." [Agreed upon]

The Prophet 🙵 in his advice to Ibn Abbas 🙲 said, "...I'hfath (remember or observe the commands of) Allah and He will Ya'hfath (direct His care at and aid) you. I'hfath Allah and you will find Him with you (by His aid, knowledge and protection). When you invoke, invoke Allah alone, and when you ask for help, ask Allah alone.

Know that if the nation (meaning mankind and the Jinn) came together to bring you benefit, they can never bring you any benefit except that which Allah has written for you. And if they came together to harm you, they will never be able to harm you, except what Allah has written for you. The pens have already been raised (and stopped writing) and the pages have dried." [Musnad Ahmad and at-Tirmidhee]

He 🙵 also said, "No Muslim supplicates to Allah with a Du'aa that does not involve sin or cutting the relations of the womb, but Allah will grant him one of the three things. He will either hasten the response to his supplication, save it for him until the Hereafter, or would turn an equivalent amount of evil away from him." They (the Sahabah 🙲) said, "What if we were to recite more (Du'aa)." He 🙵 said, "There is more with Allah." [Musnad Ahmad]

It is also stated in a Hadeeth of Allah's Messenger ﷺ, "No precaution can protect against the decree of Allah. Du'aa is beneficial with regard to what has been decreed and what has not been decreed. The Du'aa meets the calamity that has been decreed and wrestles with it, until the Day of Resurrection." [(Hasan) Saheeh al-Jamee (7739)]

"And if Allah touches you with hurt, there is none who can remove it but He, and if He intends any good for you, there is none who can repel His Favor which He causes it to reach whomsoever of His slaves He will. And He is the Oft-Forgiving, Most Merciful." [Soorah Yunus (10): 107]

Distinguishing
between
trial and
punishment

If the affliction results from acts of obedience to Allah, such as injury in struggling in the way of Allah, losing money during Hijrah (migrating for the sake of Allah), losing a job because of accepting Islam or because one attempts to follow the Sunnah of Allah's Messenger ﷺ then the affliction is a trial. Whoever bears it with patience will be rewarded and whoever exhibits annoyance will evoke the wrath of Allah upon him.

If the affliction befalls due to sinful actions, such as illnesses caused by drinking alcohol and using drugs, etc. then the affliction is a punishment from Allah. Hasten to avoid all sinful acts and turn towards Allah in repentance and ask his forgiveness. Otherwise, know that the punishments of the Hereafter are far more severe and unbearable.

If the affliction is neither connected to a good deed nor a sin such as other kinds of disease and sickness, losing a child, or failing in business, then one needs to review his actions; as calamities are in most cases a result of one's actions. Otherwise, Allah has caused this affliction to test your patience.

Allah's Messenger ﷺ said:
"One amongst the inhabitants of Hell, who had lived a life of ease and pleasure in the world would be made to dip in the Hell Fire only once on the Day of Resurrection.
Then it would be asked, 'O son of Adam, Did you find any comfort. Did you get any blessing?'
He would say, 'By Allah, no, my Lord!'
Then a person, from the inhabitants of Paradise, who had led the most miserable life would be made to dip once in Paradise and it would be said to him, 'O son of Adam, Did you face any hardship or experience any distress?'
He would say, 'By Allah! No
never have I experienced any hardship or distress."
[Saheeh Muslim (6738)]

ALWAYS REMEMBER

- Hardship and ease are a Trial for you.
- Everything Allah chooses for you; good and evil, is for your benefit.
- Whatever occurred to you could not have missed you and what missed you could never have reached you.
- Sabr (Patience) is obligatory.
- Rewards are only for those who are patient with the Decree of Allah.
- Panick and impatience cannot prevent the Decree of Allah.
- Shakwah (Complaining) is contradictory to Sabr.
- Allah Alone can protect you from harm and ease your difficulties.

CPSIA information can be obtained
at www.ICGtesting.com
Printed in the USA
BVHW050822060223
657835BV00011B/1685